Scaling Social Entrepreneurship:

Lessons Learned from One Laptop per Child

By

Robert H. Hacker

The cover image was created using a word cloud application at jasondavies.com.

The Hult Prize is an annual international case competition for university students to solve social problems through social entrepreneurship. (Photo by author)

"Creativity always comes as a surprise to us; therefore we can never count on it and we dare not believe in it until it has happened. In other words, we would not consciously engage upon tasks whose success clearly requires that creativity be forthcoming. Hence, the only way in which we can bring our creative resources fully into play is by misjudging the nature of the task, by presenting it to ourselves as more routine, simple, undemanding of genuine creativity than it will turn out to be."
Albert O. Hirschman

"There is no passion to be found playing small, in settling for a life that is less than the one you are capable of living."
Nelson Mandela

"The state, the embodiment of deliberately organized and consciously directed power, ought to be only a small part of the much richer organism which we call "society" and ... the former [state] ought to provide merely a framework within which free ...collaboration of men has the maximum scope."
F.A. Hayek

TABLE OF CONTENTS

Forward

Many people stimulated my thinking on social entrepreneurship during my years at the non-profit foundation One Laptop per Child (OLPC). Their ideas may not be fully acknowledged in this book. I would like to thank Giulia D'Amico, Mariana Cortes, Chuck Kane, Walter Bender and Miguel Brechner for their friendship, patient explanations and insights that enabled me to hopefully better understand social problems and how social entrepreneurship can be applied to achieve solutions to such problems. Chuck also arranged for me to teach a course in social entrepreneurship each January in 2011-2015 at the MIT Sloan School of Management. Richard Bernstein of Greenberg Trauriq should also be recognized for bringing me the opportunity to work for the first time in my career in the non-profit sector.

As explained in the following Introduction, a single comment by Nicholas Negroponte led me to write this book. Another comment from Nicholas may be the basis for my third book. Any errors in this book are solely my responsibility.

Many people encouraged me to write a book about OLPC. I elected not to do such a book but rather to more generally discuss the lessons I learned about how to scale a social entrepreneurship project. For more on the philosophy and history of OLPC I recommend Walter Bender and Chuck Kane's "Learning to Change the World: The Social Impact of One Laptop per Child".

This book was influenced by my appreciation for the principles of the Austrian School of Economics and Bruce Caldwell's excellent book "Hayek's Challenge: An Intellectual Biography of F.A. Hayek", which may not be credited in all instances.

Dr. Colleen Robb reviewed this book in its early draft. I would like to thank her for comments and suggestions that were instrumental in improving this book and better organizing my thoughts on social entrepreneurship.

I would like to also thank my wife, Hortensia, for putting up with my more than two hundred foreign trips over the last thirty years, which provided first hand background on the developing markets of Asia and Latin America. She also deserves most of the credit for encouraging me to write.

One cannot work on a project for children such as One Laptop without appreciating more fully the gift of our children. This book is dedicated to my daughter, Christina.

My favorite OLPC photo. West Bank 2010. Image credit:
http://laptop.org/en/children/countries/mideast.shtml

Introduction

From September 2009 until April 2013 I served as the CFO of One Laptop per Child Association. The mission of OLPC is to provide a modern education through a connected laptop to every child in the developing world. Nicholas Negroponte, Seymour Papert and several other professors and staff at the MIT Media Lab founded OLPC in 2005. Nicholas was the co-founder of the world famous MIT Media Lab and Seymour, his colleague at the Media Lab, was one of the leading authorities in the area of how to facilitate child learning through computers.

When Nicholas founded the MIT Media Lab he adopted two principles that established the culture of the organization:

1. "Demo or die"
2. "Do the impossible"

"Demo or die" basically determined the type of research that was desired. Rather than writing academic papers, students at the Media Lab were required to develop working prototypes, either physical working models or working computer code for computer-based solutions. Papert's views on constructionism and constructivism in learning probably contributed to this approach. Alan Kay and Marvin Minsky, MIT faculty members of considerable distinction, may have also influenced this tenet. "Do the Impossible" defined the types of problems that were acceptable to work on. Students were encouraged to work on large, difficult problems where the technology for a solution did not already exist. This focus on large problems is consistent with the concept in entrepreneurship to focus on large market opportunities, although at the Media Lab it was understood that the sponsors of the Media Lab would license and commercialize the new technology developed.

This orientation toward large, difficult problems guided the philosophy and development of OLPC. OLPC's mission is to provide a laptop to 1.5 billion children in primary schools throughout the world. To achieve this end OLPC needed a solution that would scale on several dimensions. In one of our occasional discussions I said to Nicholas that OLPC, although it originated as a donative non-profit, was a great example of social entrepreneurship. Nicholas responded, "social entrepreneurship does not scale." As was the case several times, Nicholas made a single statement that prompted me to go off and think about an issue—sometimes for several years—which resulted in this book. [Note: Nicholas' view of the limitations of social entrepreneurship is based on a belief that to achieve scale in solving social problems an organization had to engage national governments around the world. Such governments were much more likely to "partner" with non-profits that did not have the profit motive of an entrepreneur.]

Prior to OLPC I spent 30 years working in the private sector and twenty of those years I worked outside the U.S. I have worked in over fifty countries, mostly in Asia and Latin America, and I lived in Peru and Indonesia. One advantage of spending so much time overseas is that I was able to first hand observe a country's development over a significant period of time. With the exception of China, every country that I visited beginning in the 1980s exhibited a significant improvement in the standard of living by the start of the 21st century through the capitalist system of free enterprise. The examples I would cite to demonstrate my point would include Mexico, Singapore, Korea, Taiwan, Peru and Thailand, all of which were very undeveloped countries in the early 1980s and today are vibrant economies with a significant improvement in the standard of living. While stable governments, democracy and globalization were all contributing factors in certain countries, I see capitalism as the one common factor in the countries I cited and in many other countries. Based on my own experience I have great confidence in capitalist, for-profit companies as a way to improve peoples lives anywhere in the world and thereby address social needs.

During the financial crisis of 2008 when the world economic system reportedly came close to collapse, the issue of the morality of capitalism re-emerged as a popular topic and encouraged the growth of social entrepreneurship. History often paints capitalism as fundamentally amoral, lacking a moral system. Milton Friedman's now famous dictum that the purpose of a corporation is to maximize shareholder returns did much to popularize the absence of morality in capitalism. However, to criticize capitalism for a lack of morality based on the egregious behavior of a few individuals is comparable to criticizing the social system of "government" because of the behavior of Hitler or Stalin. It is the people operating the social system that may be immoral and generally not the system itself.

My belief that capitalism can behave morally and make a social contribution is in part based on the nine years I spent working in Indonesia. Indonesia is one of the poorest countries in Asia with per capita income of $600 or about $2 per day during most of the time I lived there (1990-1999). With a lot of other people helping, I built a billion dollar retail company in seven years that purchased $700 million dollars a year in locally manufactured merchandise, created 20,000 new retail jobs, built out one million square feet of retail space per year and was one of the largest private sector tax payers in the country. These activities had a positive social and economic benefit beyond just our employees for thousands of other workers and their families in Indonesia. No socially motivated NGO, multi-lateral bank or non-profit organization improved the number of lives we benefited operating a for-profit company. Perhaps only the Indonesian government affected more people than this private retail company. The point here is not to toot my horn but rather to show the positive impact in a poor country of a large, private, for-profit company with no explicit "social" mission.

This confidence in the capitalist system instinctively makes me suspect of the need for the adjective "social" to modify entrepreneurship. (This may be similar to the debate in microeconomics over whether "utility" needed the modifier "marginal".) "Social" to modify entrepreneurship implies that this form of entrepreneurship is more focused on societal, economic and environmental problems than traditional entrepreneurship. Also implied is the idea that creating social value is better or preferred to merely creating economic value. Setting aside the problem of how one might measure "social" value, I would question the premise that we even need a distinction for the social value component in social entrepreneurship, particularly given my experience in Indonesia.

Despite my reluctance to acknowledge "social" as a meaningful distinction in entrepreneurship, I have organized this book on social entrepreneurship to develop the following themes:

- Why social entrepreneurship emerged as a new "business model", which includes an argument for how to combine capitalism and morality as an integrated approach *(Chapter I-The Emergence of Social Entrepreneurship in the 21st Century)*
- The government's defined role as the sole provider of "public good" has been relaxed, opening the door for the private sector to provide social services *(Chapter II- Government and the Public Good)*
- The non-profit movement has influenced the development of social entrepreneurship, resulting in social entrepreneurs erroneously electing non-profits status. Such an election restricts access to capital markets (in my experience) and deprives them of a key resource to scale their organizations to address worldwide social problems *(Chapter III- Non-*

profit Foundations and Their Influence on Social Entrepreneurship)

- Social entrepreneurship can be defined in economic terms without the need for normative judgments. Using the framework of value creation-value capture, social entrepreneurship is defined basically as a decision to transfer value to the end user (the "social" benefit) rather than a shareholder *(Chapter IV- Social Entrepreneurship Defined)*

- Social entrepreneurship has three basic models where the transfer of value is coincident with an exchange (sale). To think of social entrepreneurship, as commonly defined, as combining social objectives with commercial practices is inadequate. *(Chapter V- The Three Models of Social Entrepreneurship)*

- Social entrepreneurship should address large, worldwide problems, wherein lies the requirement for scaling *(Chapter VI- Social Entrepreneurship Should Address the Large Social Problems)*

- To scale a social entrepreneurship venture (SEV), "business model" thinking provides a useful methodology or process based on my experience in both the non-profit and for-profit sectors. The parts of a business model for an SEV are described in detail with examples. *(Chapter VII- Scaling Social Entrepreneurship)*

- The opportunity for social entrepreneurship may have arisen due to the current shortcomings in capitalism and its executives, but capitalism and traditional entrepreneurship have made a significant contribution to addressing social problems worldwide. (***Chapter VIII-The Conclusions***)

Chapter I-The Emergence of Social Entrepreneurship in the 21st Century

Many believe that social entrepreneurship emerged as an alternative form of entrepreneurship in the first decade of the 21st century because more and more people were turning away from "big business" in order to "do good" and "save the world". While true for some individuals, I believe that four factors explain the emergence of social entrepreneurship:

1. A Nobel prize for Muhammad Unus
2. A renewal of the question of whether capitalism is moral
3. A wide spread recognition that government alone cannot solve social problems
4. The writings of C.K, Prahalad and Clayton Christensen

Muhammad Unus and C.K. Prahalad deserve much of the credit for the emergence of social entrepreneurship. The fact that Unus is from Bangladesh and Prahalad is from India is not a coincidence, but rather the basis for their more profound understanding of the dynamics of developing markets and their populations.

Social entrepreneurship gained international acclaim when Muhammad Unus won the Nobel Prize in 2006 for his micro-lending activities in Bangladesh. Providing loans to foster economic development for very poor people had never been done on a large scale prior to Unus' Grameen Bank. Grameen Bank is now one of the largest companies in the world using social entrepreneurship as its business model, with annual revenues in 2011 exceeding $170 million. Tom's Shoes, to be discussed in Chapter V, may indeed be larger, but I could not find any reliable information on annual revenues. The key factor to explain the success of the Unus' program was that poor people actually do repay their loans (despite belief to the contrary by many). I learned the same lesson in Indonesia in the 1990s building a credit card program for customers that earned only $1000 per year.

The economic crisis of 2007 re-opened the debate from the 1930s about the morality of capitalism and the reasons for renewed debate were the same. A period of high economic growth and significant wealth accumulation was followed by a period of major economic collapse. Such wide swings in the economy were perceived as the fault of the capitalists and their immoral behavior, as evidenced by all the average people whose lives were disrupted when the economy crashed. Faced with such stern criticism and claims of immorality, a natural outgrowth was for everyone, including for-profit corporations, to act in ways that were more socially responsible. One derivative idea was social entrepreneurship.

Harvard Business School (HBS) weighed in with several articles in support of capitalism and social responsibility. After all why do we need a business school if capitalism is doomed to collapse under the weight of its immoral behavior? Michael Porter, the world-renowned strategy professor at the school, described the situation after 2007: "The capitalist system is under siege. In recent years business increasingly has been viewed as a major cause of social, environmental, and economic problems. Companies are widely perceived to be prospering at the expense of the broader community."

Porter's solution is the concept of "shared value", which he defines as:
"... creating economic value in a way that *also* creates value for society by addressing its needs and challenges... the concept of shared value...recognizes that societal needs, not just conventional economic needs, define markets. It also recognizes that social harms or weaknesses frequently create *internal* costs for firms—such as wasted energy or raw materials, costly accidents, and the need for remedial training to compensate for inadequacies in education."[1]
 A classic example of shared value is a company that should avoid polluting a river because the pollution kills the

company's potential customers down river. If this example does not move you to reconsider the morality of capitalism, other professors at HBS offered perhaps more persuasive arguments.

Rebecca Henderson and Karthik Ramanna from HBS produced a paper titled "Managers and Market Capitalism". Long overdue, in my opinion, the authors introduce the need for morality in capitalism. The paper argues that businesses have a moral responsibility in addition to Milton Friedman's economic dictum to maximize shareholder returns. The authors argue that businesses have a moral obligation to serve society by preserving free markets and capitalism and not just satisfy the self-interest of shareholders. Essentially if capitalism and free markets were to end, the shareholders would be harmed by a significant or total loss in the value of their shareholdings. Therefore, egregious behavior, such as the 2007 financial crisis, undermines the integrity of capitalism and free markets and is therefore immoral. Although the authors did not extend the argument, I believe that they would agree that more socially responsible behavior by corporations fosters more confidence in capitalism and thereby benefits shareholders. Many argue implicitly or explicitly for the need for more social ventures, including social entrepreneurship, due to the lack of a moral compass in for-profit ventures as a result of the underlying concept of self-interest. I believe that Henderson and Ramanna present a simple logic that shows for-profit managers a reason for moral behavior—the preservation of the capitalist system. While it may not meet the standards of the Ten Commandments or other well-known moral systems, preserving the capitalist system does provide the basis to infuse capitalism with an easily understood morality—act in ways which foster an appreciation and respect for capitalism by society. All but the most die-hard communist should see value in the argument.

If not yet convinced about the role of morality in capitalism, Herbert Simon, the 1978 Nobel Prize winner in economics offers support to introduce morality in capitalism. Simon developed the concept of bounded rationality--decisions can only be optimal and never maximized. Bounded rationality offers for-profit managers the "flexibility" for considerable moral and socially beneficial behaviors to perpetuate the capitalist system. Optimal decisions are by definition a matter of interpretation and not held to the more rigorous standard of maximization. The flexibility inherent in optimal decisions offers management the opportunity for a for-profit company to act in the socially responsible and moral way proposed by Henderson and Ramanna.

Supporting a view for a larger role for the private sector in providing social services is the research of John Macomber, a lecturer at HBS. In a paper in the *Journal of Applied Corporate Finance*[2], Macomber argues that there is a significant opportunity for the private sector to invest in the world's cities. He makes three key points:

- "Over the next twenty years, the number of people living in cities will double, with three billion additional urban dwellers."
- "Shared resources like clean water, clean air, energy, and places to put solid waste are already scarce and constrained. Urbanization will only exacerbate these pressures."
- "Almost no local or national government can mobilize both the capital and the political consensus to make investments in the infrastructure that will lead to more effective use of these resources."

Macomber concludes:

"There is a largely unrecognized opportunity for the private sector to engage in selective investments that consider these [three] trends. Investors and entrepreneurs can make money by extending these "common good" kinds of items, which use resources more productively. In the winning situations, this makes these cities more economically competitive at the same time. "

Macomber's "common good" can be used interchangeably with what many economists refer to as the "public good".

If this argument applies to cities, the logical extension of it is to realize that on a cumulative basis it also applies at the country level. National governments are equally unable to address social problems for the same reasons as their cities, but national governments face the even more challenging issue of trying to serve the rural populous where resources are scarce and many of the poor live.

Deutsche Bank, the financial services giant, appears to share the view of Macomber. Citing logic similar to the scholar, Deutsche Bank has identified a strategic investment opportunity for the private sector in cities to improve education and build new infrastructure. Implicitly, Deutsche Bank is saying that financing private sector providers of social services in cities is a better social and economic investment than financing the municipality itself. This strategic priority for Deutsche Bank might also be considered an endorsement of social entrepreneurship or the shared value concept of Porter. Stretching the argument, Deutsche

Bank could be giving many governments a vote of "no confidence".

Another academic who shares a concern for government's ability to address social problems is William Duggan, a strategy professor at my alma mater, Columbia University Graduate School of Business. In his excellent book, "Strategic Intuition: The Creative Spark in Human Achievement", Duggan argues that the failure by the government to solve social problems has prompted the private sector to address social problems in the U.S. Duggan also believes that the phenomenal success of businesses in the last twenty years, citing Google, Microsoft and IBM as examples, has prompted people to consider using for-profit business management techniques to address social problems. One example to support this argument is social entrepreneurship.

Another factor that contributes to the increased focus on the poor and disadvantaged is simple capitalism. The developed markets were fully exploited as a market opportunity in the 50-60 years after WWII. What is a for-profit company, such as Proctor & Gamble or General Foods, to do to insure growth in revenue and profit? One choice is to move down market and either intentionally or inadvertently serve the poorer and disadvantaged customers in the third world.

The strategy of serving the disadvantaged was perhaps first explained by C.K. Prahalad in his 2004 book, *"The Fortune at the Bottom of the Pyramid: Eradicating Poverty through Profits"*. Prahalad argues that by developing products customized to the social and economic requirements of people living on $1-2 per day, companies could profitably develop large, new markets. To achieve the price points demanded by Prahalad's strategy, new business models were required to achieve sustainable operations. Social entrepreneurship with its lower product margins and overheads emerged as one business model to serve the "bottom of the pyramid".

Clayton Christensen is another distinguished professor from HBS who supports the view of serving underserved markets. Christensen studies innovation. He argues that one does not size a market by looking at the number of units being sold. Rather, the number of people who cannot afford the product really determines the market potential. By reformulating a product or service with a more limited feature set at a lower price a new market can be developed for the under served. One example of the under served is the poor, or Prahalad's "bottom of the pyramid". Christensen's logic encourages the capitalist to look down market into the poorer markets of the under served for new revenue opportunities. The proliferation of cheap cell phones and cellular service in developing countries may be an example to illustrate Christensen's point.

The writing of Prahalad and Christensen helped to make people more aware of the underserved and the techniques that could be used to serve these people profitably. The poor person does not care whether it is a non-profit foundation, a social entrepreneur, Proctor & Gamble, or the late Mother Theresa for that matter, who provides their toothpaste, medicine, or clean water at an affordable price.

Many believe that government has the primary responsibility to solve social problems. This modern thinking was perhaps exemplified by Franklin Delano Roosevelt's presidential efforts to establish the New Deal in the 1930s. Roosevelt's thinking was based on a new interpretation of the U.S. constitution according to certain legal scholars.[3] Rather than interpreting the constitution as defining what was permitted, Roosevelt acted on the basis that if the constitution did not prohibit it, then new legislation to expand government's role was permitted. Roosevelt perhaps derived his view of government from the 19th century German philosopher Otto Neurath, who some credit with first proposing the government as the provider of the "welfare state".[4] In fairness to both Roosevelt and Neurath, the politically charged "welfare state" is really nothing more than a debate about the role of government and perhaps central planning by government. The role of government in a certain sense defines the boundary after which capitalism and social entrepreneurship are free to operate. One interesting benefit, in my opinion, of the popularity of social entrepreneurship is that it may help to reduce the role of government or foster a better quality of debate on what role government should play in addressing social issues.

This way of thinking about the role of government was reinforced by the writings of John Maynard Keynes beginning in 1936. According to Fredrich Hayek, the Nobel Laureate economist, Keynes saw active policies by the government to stimulate economic demand as the logical extension of the success of a bigger government in successfully winning WWII. If an expanded government could successfully prosecute WWII, then such an approach could and should be applied to domestic economic and social problems. The expanded role of government laid the foundation for an expansion of the concept of "public good" and perhaps served as an example for many other governments around the world.

Henry B. Hansmann in his 1980 *Yale Law Journal* article, "The Role of Non-profit Enterprise", defines the public good in economic terms as that which:

(1) Costs no more to provide the good to one or to many

(2) [Any] one person's enjoyment of the good does not interfere with another person's enjoyment

Weisbrod (1977) theorizes that the public good has two additional characteristics:

(1) They are "nonrival" in the sense that an individual's consumption of them does not affect the consumption by another

(2) They are "nonexcludable" in the sense that individuals who fail to pay for them cannot be excluded from their consumption.

Weibrod's inclusion of "nonexcludable" is a significant expansion of the scope of the definition of public good presented by Hansmann and more broadly defines it to better match the services many have come to expect from government.

Traditional examples of public good include education, healthcare, public transportation and law enforcement. Many economists, including Hayek, have argued that it is the role of government to provide certain services as the public good. For example, Hayek advocated for primary school education as a public good. Other Nobel Laureate economists, such as Milton Friedman, have argued that certain "public goods" should be provided by the private sector. Charter schools would be an example. This divergence of opinion and government budget constraints have in part left open the opportunity to for-profits to fill the role of "public good" providers and encouraged the development of social entrepreneurship.

Despite Roosevelt and Keynes setting the stage for government to provide an expanded public good, few if any governments are effectively addressing the large, worldwide social problems. Many governments are members of the United Nations and shareholders in the multi-lateral development banks such as Inter-American Development Bank or World Bank ("multi-laterals"), but in the end "all politics is local" and few voters place higher priority on worldwide social problems than local or domestic issues.

When we examine government efforts to address domestic social issues we encounter two problems with government programs:

1. With the possible exception of national defense, domestic law enforcement and management of judicial systems, national governments may not be able to consistently demonstrate any world-class, "best practices" in management. Therefore, government may not be efficient in its management of most problems. The failure of twentieth century centralized communist governments is perhaps the best proof of this

point. The higher costs of care in government run hospitals in the U.S. compared with private hospitals also support this conclusion.

2. Government approaches and solutions tend not to focus on the end user problem. Governments typically cater to the re-election plans of sitting officials, voters (e.g. parents) and politically powerful lobbying groups (e.g. private sector suppliers and unions). For example, the current federal and state government efforts to improve education in U.S. public schools focuses on test results, teacher development and technology infrastructure for classrooms. Not a single resource devoted to these efforts directly impacts a child or student. The student has the "problem" that needs to be solved—improved learning. Most parents in my experience can talk about how their children learn, but this primary focus is lost when the government gets involved. I believe an examination of public healthcare leads to the same conclusions, as demonstrated by the number of people each year who leave their country and its public healthcare system to seek treatment in privately owned hospitals in other countries.

The shortcomings of a government to effectively serve the public good domestically in part may also explain their inability to effectively participate in solutions to worldwide social problems.

So, if governments cannot effectively shoulder the burden of solving global social issues, who can?

Chapter III- Non-profit Foundations and Their Influence on Social Entrepreneurship

While government's ability to serve the public good and provide social services should probably always have been in question, one response to the underserved needs of society was met in part through non-profit foundations. Non-profit organizations for social purposes date back several centuries. One of the first efforts to legally codify such matters was in England in 1602[5]. An historian might cite earlier efforts to formalize non-profit activities, perhaps looking at collectives, guilds or buying groups. The long history of foundations and the provision of social services also had a profound effect on how people think about social entrepreneurship and many SEVs elect non-profit status as their legal form of organization. Whether or not that is the best choice will be discussed in this and later chapters.

We return to Hansmann (1980) for a comprehensive definition of the non-profit foundation. To summarize Hansmann, non-profits typically have four characteristics:

1. They do not distribute excess cash flow to stakeholders
2. They serve the "public good"
3. They subsidize the consumption of others
4. They maintain a "trust" in the non-distribution constraint

Hansmann's first characteristic of a non-profit is that by their selection of a particular form of organization under the tax code (in the U.S.), they are barred from returning any excess cash flow to individuals who exercise control such as officers, directors or trustees. Any excess cash flow must be re-invested in assets to provide the services of the non-profit or in the operating activities of the organization.

Hansmann second characteristic, the definition of the public good, was explained in the last chapter.

Non-profits are traditionally subsidy providers, lowering the cost of a product or service or offering them for free to those who cannot pay market prices. By not having the motivation and contractual obligation to provide a return to shareholders, non-profits are free to lower margins or provide the goods and services at below cost (including for free), thereby using their funding to provide the subsidy to the presumed less fortunate. Non-profits as subsidy providers also explain funding for certain performing arts, where the demand for performances is too small to justify a for-profit company providing the service. Another example may be donations to educational institutions where the donations subsidize scholarships that cannot be made from the educational institution's cash flow or from government support.

Hansmann's last characteristic of a non-profit is perhaps the most insightful and provides an understanding of a real service provided by non-profits. Non-profits serve as "trustees" for their donors. Much of serving the public good is difficult to monitor, particularly when the activities are across the world in Asia or Africa. Non-profits have no incentive not to provide their service and no incentive except to provide their product or service at the lowest cost possible. A for profit company seeking return for shareholders might not send all the food to the needy children in Africa or might overstate the cost of the food to enrich shareholders, but Hansmann believes that non-profits have no such self-interest.

While many would laud non-profits for their lack of self-interest, I think the professed absence of self-interest is the shortcoming in non-profits and perhaps one of the reasons that the social entrepreneurship venture has emerged as a viable alternative to execute social projects.

The absence of self-interest in non-profits causes two problems for non-profits:

1. There is no incentive for non-profits to be efficient.

   It is widely recognized in economic theory that every exchange of a product or service is based on each party believing that the exchange serves their self-interest. The provider of the product or service achieves this end by operating as efficiently as possible and by charging as much as the purchaser will bear. However, the non-profit is subsidizing the purchaser price and thereby distorting the market determination of price. With the market price distorted the incentive to be an efficient producer becomes distorted as well and may lead to less attention to operating efficiency. Hansmann makes the same point differently[6]: "It is almost certainly true that nonprofit firms are productively inefficient in the sense that...they will generally produce any good or service at a higher cost than would a for-profit firm. If it were otherwise, we would expect to find non-profits operating in a much broader range of industries than is actually the case."

   Complaints over the last several years about the high percentage of administrative costs in non-profit foundations might support this conclusion.

2. There is no incentive for non-profits to scale their operations

   There are approximately 1.5 million non-profit organizations in the U.S., roughly one for every four tax paying corporations. The average non-profit had annual revenues in 2011 of $1.1 million and two percent have revenues over $10 million[7]. Why are the non-profits so small in terms of scale? Non-profits do not have the incentive of self-interest from the derived economic benefits of scaling. In fact, I believe self-interest leads to the proliferation of small non-profits. Many people do not want to "anonymously" contribute to a large foundation like the Gates Foundation that is tackling the large problems on a worldwide scale. People apparently prefer to get the personal recognition of establishing their own small non-profit foundation. In certain communities it has become a status symbol to say you have a foundation. While personally satisfying, small foundations typically provide only incremental solutions and rarely address the big social problems that require scale of operations. Some would argue that there is a place for small foundations and that in some communities they aggregate resources in order to achieve economies of scale, etc. However, foundations aggregating resources are rare. Many small, stand alone foundations effectively duplicate overhead where such financial resources could be me more efficiently deployed to address the actual social problems.

When we examine the industries in which non-profits operate we recognize that they are generally similar to small business industries, industries that can achieve positive cash flow without any significant scaling. Otherwise, non-profits might be operating steel mills and building automobiles or conducting mining operations in Chile. The industries of small business and non-profits are typically also less capital intensive and therefore do not need access to capital markets to fund investment in new facilities or significant working capital requirements. A recent trend is for non-profit hospitals to convert to for-profit tax status or be acquired by for-profit hospital chains. Such moves are prompted by the need to expand their facilities or locations and achieve better economies of scale. These moves also give the organizations better access to expansion capital, which demonstrates a shortcoming in non-profit status.

Foundations require capital or expansion capital when they address large-scale worldwide problems. While historically foundations have operated with the characteristics of small businesses, as described earlier, tackling worldwide problems requires large amounts of capital to build international partnerships and distribution, to fund working capital and to fund continued innovation in product or service. In my experience commercial banks and investment banks will not finance a non-profit regardless of the scale of its revenues and cash flow. For example, almost every leading bank in the world I approached to commercially finance OLPC, despite annual revenues approaching $100 million and positive cash flow, turned me down. If the objective is to address large, worldwide social problems, access to commercial capital markets is required and the organization should elect to be a for-profit corporation rather than a non-profit foundation.

It may be noted at this point that there has been no mention of the word "donations". It should also be pointed out that Hansmann made no use of donations in his definition at the beginning of this discussion of non-profit foundations. Foundations that rely principally on donations are called "donative foundations". Foundations that rely on sales of product for cash flow may in certain cases be described as SEVs, as later explained in the discussion of the three forms of social entrepreneurship. Interestingly, at a recent speech to over 100 executives from non-profit organizations, when I asked them why they were non-profits they all answered, "to receive tax deductible donations". This is what I call the "default" answer for a social organization. If you do not think about it, your social venture defaults to being a non-profit and accepts donations.

There are four possible reasons to actively select non-profit status:

1. Access to capital not available in commercial markets
   Certain projects cannot easily be financed in the commercial financial markets. Museums and performing art centers would be the two most common examples. These types of projects cannot create sufficient cash flow to attract loans and equity investors. Therefore, they can only be created and funded through donations to non-profit foundations.

2. Lower costs through volunteer communities
   Certain projects need to use the free labor of volunteers in order to be self-sustaining on a cash flow basis. For example, OLPC probably would have needed $20-30 million in additional donations to develop Sugar, the educational software on the OLPC laptop. A worldwide community of volunteers has created over 300 educational Sugar apps.

3. Partnering with NGOs, governments, multi-laterals and universities
   Certain social projects believe that they need to partner with NGOs (non-governmental organizations), governments,

multi-laterals and universities in order to achieve their social objectives. The large NGOs and multi-lateral organizations have a wealth of experience in social issues, staff across the globe with local knowledge and resources that can be leveraged to achieve more effective operations. These types of organizations are all non-profit friendly and share concerns to differing degrees about the "self-interest" of the private sector. Therefore, it may be easier to partner with multi-laterals and NGOs if the organization is a non-profit foundation.

4. Branding

   Branding, defined as, "product positioning and messaging in order to achieve emotional engagement with the user for eventual economic benefit to the seller", can be enhanced by non-profit status. For example, if the social venture is communicating a "low cost" solution, non-profit status implicitly communicates lower margins and prices.

   While these four benefits to non-profit status may be attractive, a for-profit company can also achieve all of these benefits. A deliberate review of a new organization's social mission and strategy should include a methodical analysis of whether the organization's objectives are better served by non-profit or for-profit status. Unless the social project cannot generate sufficient cash flow to access capital markets, such as museums and performing arts centers, I recommend for-profit social entrepreneurship rather than a non-profit foundation.

Chapter IV- Social Entrepreneurship Defined

Much academic literature has been devoted to defining social entrepreneurship. In a 2011 paper, "A Conceptual Overview of What We Know About Social Entrepreneurship"[8], Hoogendoorn outlines four definitions of social entrepreneurship that date back to 1998[9]. The four definitions are:

1. Non-profit organizations that apply business expertise to become more efficient in providing and delivering their social services
2. For-profit businesses run by non-profits to help offset costs and become independent from grants and subsidies
3. High donor control philanthropy, where donors pursue their own personal social vision
4. Socially responsible businesses that offer innovative solutions to persistent social, economic, and ecological problems using market-based models

Hoogendoorn believes these four definitions share a common characteristic:

"The [four] approaches ... share one main commonality: their emphasis on the creation of social value. While it is a long-held belief that entrepreneurs contribute positively to society, it is motivation and the relative importance of social value creation [as opposed to economic value creation] that distinguishes social entrepreneurs from commercial entrepreneurs"

Underlying Hoogendoorn's concept of social value is an assumption that social value is somehow determined by a normative judgment. Such normative judgment enables one to determine the "relative importance" of social entrepreneurship compared with traditional entrepreneurship. Social value is perceived as somehow better than economic value. However, as Felipe Santos[10] points out:

"Such articulations [social value] are problematic ... because they require subjective assessments about who is in need of "social help" and suggest that profit cannot or should not be an outcome of fulfilling those needs. They also assume that there is some form of metric or set of values that make certain types of value creation "social" and others not. "

While Hoogendoorn and many other scholars acknowledge the social contribution of commercial activities and entrepreneurship, they consistently return to the concepts of social mission, social change, social impact and the implied "greater value" in social entrepreneurship. However, it is questionable that this distinction survives the scrutiny of economists. What meaningful difference is there between inner city schools whether they be charter schools, public schools or Catholic parish schools? Each school serves the same disadvantaged children and only their funding mechanism and the economic benefit derived for the sponsors of the school is different. In the end, it is the same children who need to be educated, the same "social mission" and presumably the same "social value" achieved through each type of school. This, of course, assumes that this nebulous notion of social value is not somehow reduced in the case of the parish or charter school by the simple desire to generate sufficient cash flow or a return to stakeholders. Aside perhaps from certain communists, I see no ideology that would reduce the "social value" of the three school alternatives based on economic returns. One could argue that the schools that require some targeted cash flow or profit could reduce the targets and direct those additional funds to benefit the children. Parish and charter schools fill a void in the market for education that some governmental authority decided needed to be filled. These forms of schools were presumably the best alternative the licensing authorities had. The licensing authorities deemed the level of service for the children and their families to be satisfactory or better regardless of the cash flow targets of the operators.

All corporations produce an economic value that has social benefit as Hoogendoorn acknowledges. The sum of the benefits derived by the individuals is the benefit to society or "social" value[11]. If we accept this simple premise, we avoid the trap of normative judgment surrounding social value and are free to discuss social entrepreneurship in purely economic terms.

First I should make clear that value in economic terms is defined as utility. The Austrian school of economics first introduced the concept of utility as the measurement of value. Prior to the Austrian School's insight, the value of a product could be paraphrased as the sum of three factors-- the cost of inputs, the cost of labor and the return to the investor. The profound insight that the Austrians brought to the definition of value was the concept of customer perception or subjectivism. Value was also a function of each customer's perception of value in terms of pleasure, satisfaction and happiness. Therefore, value was relative and not only the sum of the three factors.

With value defined, we now move on to applying the concept to define social entrepreneurship. However, first we need to make a distinction between value creation and value capture. This distinction was first introduced by Bowman and Ambrosini in their 2002 paper "Value Creation Versus Value Capture: Towards a Coherent Definition of Value in Strategy". Value creation is none other than the utility to the customer or user[12]. Value capture is the monetization that takes place in the exchange between the goods or services provider and the user or consumer. In other words, value capture is the cash or consideration paid when someone elects to purchase a good or service based on their perception of value.

Felipe Santos, a Professor at INSEAD[13], used the value creation-value capture framework to define social entrepreneurship. Social entrepreneurs maximize value creation and satisfices for value capture. Effectively, the social entrepreneur transfers as much value as possible to the user, provided the economic consideration received is sufficient to sustain operating cash flow. In contrast, a traditional entrepreneur satisfices for value creation, which is required by definition for a self-interested exchange to take place, and tries to maximize the value capture. Maximizing for value capture is just a different way of stating Milton Friedman's maxim that a corporation should maximize shareholder return. In summary, social entrepreneurs maximize value creation and traditional entrepreneurs maximize value capture. Effectively, social entrepreneurship becomes a strategic or economic decision on what level of margins and resultant cash flow is targeted with no need for any normative judgments. Social entrepreneurship is nothing more than a decision for how to share value, with the end user being the preferred beneficiary rather than a shareholder. It should be pointed out that this definition works regardless of the form of legal organization (non-profit-501(c)3, 501(c)4, for- profit-C corporation, S corporation, B corporation, LLC, etc.) adopted by the SEV, provided the organization has a self-sustaining cash flow.

The concept of value proposition, a fundamental concept in entrepreneurship, provides another way to think about value creation. A value proposition is the unique [competitive] set of economic and emotional benefits of a product or service for a targeted customer such that an economic exchange takes place. The value proposition assumes a defined target market. Therefore, the value proposition must provide sufficient benefits for an exchange to take place with the end users in the target market, which then permits scaling in markets of a large size. Any benefits to the user beyond the necessary requirement are an effort to maximize the benefits and value creation. Therefore, in social entrepreneurship the value proposition is defined to surpass the necessary benefits for an exchange and maximize. With such a definition in mind, the decision to serve the disadvantaged or poor becomes simply a decision about a target market with no need for normative judgments.

I sometimes think that social entrepreneurship might be better described as "shared entrepreneurship". A social entrepreneur must first set a price at which a self-interested exchange takes place. However, this price need only be sufficient for the resulting margins (gross margin and operating margin) to provide sufficient cash flow for the organization to be self-sustaining and invest in future development. The social entrepreneur forgoes any price (at which an exchange could take place) higher than required for self-sustainability. By foregoing the higher price, the entrepreneur is sharing the "excess" value with the end user, increasing the value to the end user and thereby maximizing value creation for the end user.

Perhaps the challenge in applying the value creation-value capture framework is in determining where an organization is on the value capture dimension with the choices simply defined as—ignore, satisfice or maximize. First we must remember that the recipients or purchasers of goods and services determine the value created and not the mission statement of an organization or a group of charitable donors. We know that one group of companies--traditional for profits--maximizes value capture in order to enrich their shareholders and only transfer sufficient value (value creation) to insure an exchange. If the organization is not pursuing the objective of maximum value capture, the organization by default should be satisficing for value capture and therefore an SEV (ignoring mismanagement and mispricing as irrational). One could argue that if the customer "sets" the exchange price then all exchanges by definition are satisficing for value capture. First, there could be a higher price at which the exchange could take place but the organization decided to offer the product at a lower price. Secondly, most products have standard ranges for gross margin everywhere in the world based on similar risk-return expectations from shareholders. If a price is set such that the gross margin is below this standard range then rationally the organization has decided not to maximize value capture and must be satisficing or irrational. If the organization ignores value capture and gives the product for free with no consideration received, there is no economic exchange.

Therefore, this organization is not participating in a commercial activity and cannot be an SEV. Such an organization is hopefully operating as a donative non-profit.

Another scenario to consider is an SEV that also receives donations either to achieve cash flow sustainability or to finance a project that cannot be done through its own cash flow. In both cases I would argue that the organization is not an SEV because they cannot sustain operations from the cash flow generated by exchange or sale. Such a scenario, the combination of donations and operating cash flow, is the most dangerous for the ongoing viability of the organization. The organization has to focus on two critical activities—operations and fundraising—which divides senior management attention. Perhaps more important, the need for donations is an explicit recognition that the business model is not self-sustaining. Trapped in its status as a non-profit in order to accept the needed donations, the organization has many fewer alternatives than a for-profit SEV that can access capital markets.

In my experience, the value creation, value capture framework also potentially contributes to better management of the SEV. One group of managers focus on the social objectives, sharing the value created. Another group of managers focus on the commercial activities and value capture. The social management team focuses on increasing value, perhaps, by example, adding training capabilities for end users, educating end users or producing project evaluation schemes. The commercial team focuses on offsetting these costs by reducing overhead, negotiating better supply agreements and arranging subsidized product distribution, to cite a few examples. I have found socially focused and commercially focused managers do not always mix well. By consciously dividing the value creation team from the team responsible for value capture the management conflicts can be reduced.

At this point, thinking as a well-schooled economist, you might be asking why would any rational investor invest in an SEV and forego the maximum returns required by Friedman? Using portfolio theory provides an insight.

An investment in an SEV is today[14] typically done at below market rates of return. The expected return is insufficient compared to alternative investments with a similar risk determination. An investment in an SEV has two components.

1. An investment that hopefully generates a return sufficient to preserve the real value of money; and

2. A "donation" that lowers the cash return to below "market"

Why does the investor not just select an investment that generates a real market return and then make a separate donation? The answer is that through an SEV the rational investor should be seeking greater operating efficiency from the donation than an alternative stand-alone donation. The efficiency of the "donation" represents the economic benefit for investing in social entrepreneurship and for the investor to forego a direct donation. For example, an investor could pay for and build homes for the needy. Alternatively, the investor could donate to an SEV building homes (similar to Habitat for Humanity) where the scale of the project hopefully lowers costs and thereby provides more housing units (and social benefit) to the needy. This desire by the investor for efficiency in the "donation" to the SEV brings us to the key question of how to scale the SEV to achieve economies of scale and significant impact on social problems. However, before I talk about scaling I need to first discuss the three models of social entrepreneurship.

Chapter V- The Three Models of Social Entrepreneurship

In examining the models of social entrepreneurship, SEVs share one characteristic--the value capture is coincident with the value creation at the time the product or service is provided. There is no delay between providing (creating) the value and receiving the compensation. An example may illustrate my point. A non-profit foundation sells tchotchkes - coffee cups, calendars, scarves etc. - and uses the profits from this activity to underwrite the cost of a program to provide free eyeglasses to children in Africa. The economic exchange is the sale of the tchotchkes, but this sale does not take place at the time the African children receive their eyeglasses. The value creation for the children is not a result of the value capture of the tchotchkes sale. Without the linkage of the value creation and value capture there is no social entrepreneurship. In other words, the entrepreneurship provides the solution to a problem rather than funds the solution. Of course, the children in Africa would still benefit from the foundation's "business model". It is just not social entrepreneurship. A benefit of my restrictive definition is that we can simply focus on entrepreneurship and finding new users with problems to be solved, rather than develop new approaches to corporate social responsibility or new concepts such as Porter's shared value.

In social entrepreneurship the requirement that value creation and value capture be coincident suggests three business models. The models are:

1. BOGO (buy one, give one)

   In the BOGO Model coincident with the value capture (sale of a product) another unit of the product is given free to someone in need thereby creating additional social benefit. The free unit represents the surplus value foregone by the organization and transferred to social benefit for the recipient. An outstanding example of this business model is TOMS Shoes.

2. The Sales Model

   In the Sales Model the act of monetization takes place at the point in time when the social value is delivered. OLPC is a great example of this model where every time OLPC sells a laptop to a government a child receives a free computer. The value creation is enhanced by the free services provided by OLPC to the government in areas such as teacher training and community development, which by design benefit the children.

3. The Exchange Model

   In the Exchange Model financial intermediaries, such as -
   finance organizations, lend money to people who normally
   would not have access to traditional financial institutions in
   order for the borrowers to purchase a product or service that
   will hopefully enable them to be more economically viable.
   Vittana is an excellent example of this model.

   The following material describes more fully each of the
   companies cited above.

BOGO model: TOMS Shoes (TOMS)

TOMS, founded in 2006 and headquartered in Santa Monica,
CA, is a for-profit web-based seller of contemporary, fashion
footwear for men, women and children. TOMS describes
themselves:

"TOMS Shoes was founded on a simple premise: With every
pair you purchase, TOMS will give a pair of new shoes to a
child in need. One for One. Using the purchasing power of
individuals to benefit the greater good is what we're all
about."

TOMS value proposition to the customer is based on the
BOGO model. BOGO tells the customer upfront that for every
purchase, the seller will give like kind to a person in need.

Sometimes in a BOGO model the given product is identical to the product purchased and sometimes the product is different but of sufficient quality to be responsive to the social need.

In the case of TOMS the business activities are inseparable from the social project and the BOGO model is a significant part of the brand image and value proposition for the customer. For the social project to succeed, the business must first succeed and be profitable to insure its existence. In the next example, OLPC, there is no profit making business, but the success of the "commercial" activities enables the organization to achieve its social mission.

Sales Model: One Laptop Per Child (OLPC)

OLPC is a non-profit foundation dedicated to providing a free laptop to children in the developing world to improve their education. In its early days OLPC used the BOGO model and charitable contributions to secure the laptops for donation to the children. In 2007, under the direction of then President Charles Kane, OLPC began to sell its laptops to governments who in turn gave the laptops for free to children. The principal activity of OLPC now involves a worldwide effort to sell the computers to governments, foundations and for-profit corporations interested in child education. Effectively,

OLPC is fulfilling its social mission by selling the computers provided the purchaser agrees to give the computers to every child in a community for free and follow certain other principles.

Exchange Model: Vittana

Vittana, headquartered in Seattle, WA, is a non-profit foundation that provides a website-based exchange whereby interested lenders are enabled to provide micro-finance loans to students worldwide to pay for their education. Vittana describes itself as follows:

'Vittana is an early-stage non-profit startup bringing student loans to the developing world through the power of person-to-person microfinance... we just happen to be in the business of creating good instead of creating money."

Effectively, Vittana brings together individuals interested to finance the education of students outside the U.S. and the students who need funding. Vittana provides the back office administrative processing for the lenders but outsources the in country lending and administration to independent companies approved by Vittana who specialize in micro-lending.

Another outstanding example of the exchange model is Living Goods, based in Uganda. However, Living Goods may be an example of a hybrid model that incorporates both the Vittana and OLPC's models. Living Goods provides loans to needy women (Exchange Model) to purchase health kits that they sell to the community (Sale Model) to improve healthcare and thereby earn a living. Through this hybrid model Living Good is responsible for two value creations, jobs for the sales force and better healthcare, and two values captures--the loan repayment and the sale proceeds from the health kit. I like this hybrid model and hope others will consider opportunities to use it in the developing world to achieve double social benefits— fostering self-sustaining individuals through micro-finance and the sale of socially beneficial products and services by the borrowers.

Note: Each of the organizations used as examples in this chapter have more sophisticated business models than I have described here. These models involve more complex value propositions, communities akin to what we see in social media sites and many other features. I have intentionally elected not to describe them more fully in order to hopefully make clear the fundamental concept of each model.

Two other examples may help the understanding of SEVs. A for-profit company dedicates five percent of pre-tax profit to social projects, such as many of the Fortune 500 companies headquartered in Minneapolis, MN do. A variation on this theme might be a for-profit company that dedicates a portion of net income to their foundation for social purposes. Is either example an SEV? The answer is no. The reason is that the value creation in the social projects is not coincident with the value capture—the commercial activities of the company. A common variation on this example is a coffee company that trains indigenous people to grow and treat their coffee so the coffee company pays a higher price for the coffee and supports local employment. Another way to share the value of a social benefit is a software company that requires that all employees devote twenty five percent of their time to supporting organizations devoted to social programs. All of these examples share value that has a social benefit, effectively reducing the value captured, but the beneficial activities are not coincident with the transaction with the end user and therefore not social entrepreneurship. I do think that these last two examples would be great models of how for-profit companies could genuinely demonstrate their concern for social problems.

Another example further expands the understanding of social entrepreneurship. A for-profit company makes a medical device that physically changes the male anatomy to reduce the likelihood of transferring the HIV virus during sexual intercourse (a real company but the more graphic details are intentionally omitted). The company distributes the product through traditional commercial channels and intentionally does not market to governments or multi-lateral organizations such as the United Nations. Is this company an SEV? Again, no. There is no maximizing of value creation. The company only creates sufficient value to consummate a sale or satisfices for value creation and any additional value is captured for the shareholders. Despite a large-scale operation with revenues in the hundreds of millions and a meaningful contribution to AIDS prevention, this company is not an SEV. Of course, with this company's scale and significant social benefit it does make clear again that for-profits can be used as an alternative to SEVs or foundations to achieve social objectives.

Speaking of scale, we now turn to the subject of how to scale an SEV. By this point in the book I have hopefully made clear that I view entrepreneurship as a provider of social benefits with no need for normative judgments. Therefore, the discussion of scaling an SEV uses traditional concepts from entrepreneurship and the key concept of "business model".

Chapter VI- Social Entrepreneurship Should Address the Large Social Problems

Social problems range from abandoned dogs, shelters for battered women and the need for inner-city schools in our local communities to eradicating malaria, saving the rain forests or educating all the children in the world. The UN Millennium Development Goals (MDG) provide a basis for defining the large social problems, problems that occur all over the world and create huge social, economic and political hardship for a very large number of people. The current MDG are shown below.

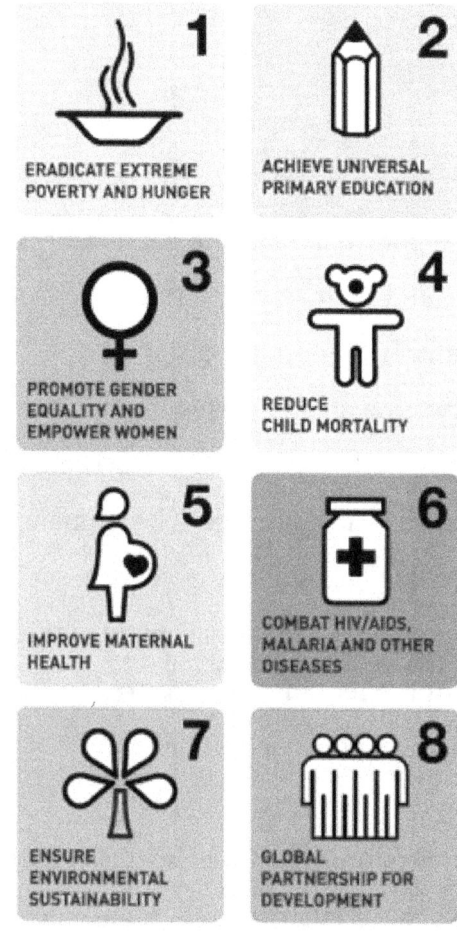

Summarizing these goals leads to a classification of the large social problems as:

1. Healthcare
2. Food and water

3. Education

4. Environment

5. Human rights

I might argue that this list omits shelter, which is a significant problem for the poor in all but the most temperate climates. These problems lend themselves to market-based solutions through social entrepreneurship, although personally I am stymied by how it can be used to address human rights. Perhaps if foundations, entrepreneurs and corporations refused to "invest" in countries with human rights violations that might bring about the necessary social change, but too many corporations and governments ignore United Nations boycotts and other similar measures to give me much confidence in such an approach.

I believe that social entrepreneurship should be directed to solving the large social problems such as those identified by the UN. The question that you may be asking is why. For the answer I turn to classical thinking on entrepreneurship. The theory of entrepreneurship says that we should tackle the large problems because they represent the largest market opportunities. The theory also says that it is just as much work in terms of time and personal energy to solve a small problem as a larger one. Therefore, the "rational" (efficient and effective) person would work on the larger problem(s) that represent the greatest opportunity.

Another argument for tackling the big problems is that the population in the developing world will reach approximately 4 billion by the beginning of the 22nd century and the population in the least developed countries [60] will total an additional 3 billion, according to the United Nations Population Division.[15] This population represents an almost threefold increase in the population of the most disadvantaged people in the one hundred year period 2000-2100. Incremental, small-scale solutions now will have no meaningful affect given the sheer number of people disenfranchised.

Yet another argument for tackling the large, worldwide problems is that it is more efficient. If we look at Brazil, for example, a different social organization could address the problem of healthcare in each of Brazils five largest cities. Each foundation or SEV would be required to pay for their staff, office space and other administrative costs. Combining the five organizations into one, larger organization would save most of the duplicated costs and free up funds to be used for the individuals in need. As an aside, this organization would have limited marginal cost to expand into other cities in Brazil … and Uruguay and Paraguay. .

While I believe that social entrepreneurship is an effective way to address large social problems, I would point out that there are two other alternatives. One alternative would be for for-profit corporations to use their bountiful excess cash to expand their corporate social responsibility. As this slide from a Michael Porter *Ted Talk* makes clear, the vast majority of annual revenue in the United States is in the hands of the private sector.

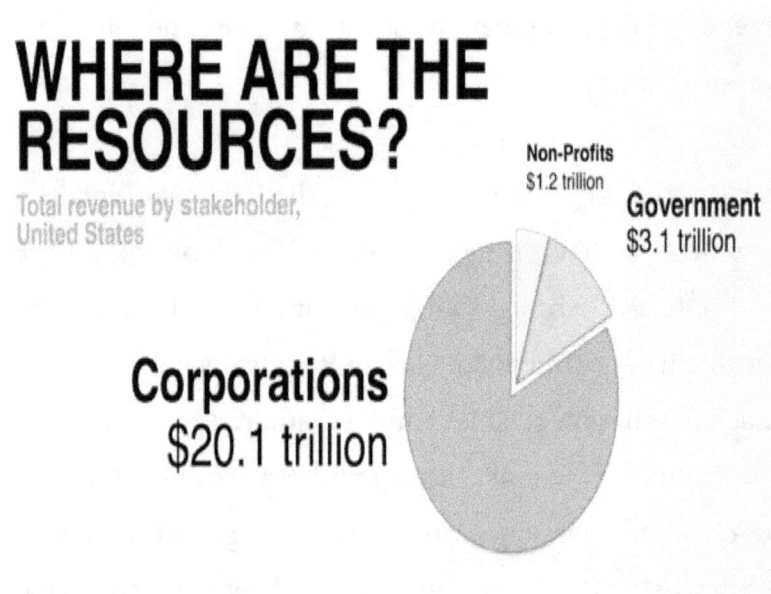

WHERE ARE THE RESOURCES?

Total revenue by stakeholder, United States

Non-Profits
$1.2 trillion

Government
$3.1 trillion

Corporations
$20.1 trillion

If only one percent of annual corporate revenue, $200 billion, were devoted to worldwide social problems, it would have no meaningful affect on corporate profits and, for example, would fund a free tablet with educational software for all 1.5 billion children in the developing world.

Worldwide problems require millions of participants to address the problems. The most effective way to create millions of participants is to properly educate the children of the world. This may really be the only effective way to create enough properly prepared individuals to address the problems. Governments, multi-laterals and corporations are trying to solve the problems but the sheer scale suggests that individual empowerment through education may be the only realistic alternative. An excellent organization that shares this point of view is DESIGN FOR CHANGE, who describes themselves as "the largest global movement designed to give children an opportunity to express their own ideas for a better world and put them into action".

The remainder of the book is devoted to practical advice on scaling social entrepreneurship to solve large, worldwide social problems. I believe the lessons are also useful for those who prefer to address local or different social problems. I do not make any value judgment about people who address these types of social problems and I encourage such efforts. I just think it is a more interesting question to explore how to solve worldwide problems through the scaling of social entrepreneurship.

Chapter VII- Scaling Social Entrepreneurship

Much of my thinking on scaling an SEV is influenced by the time I spent at OLPC where I made more than twenty foreign trips per year to developing countries to meet with potential project sponsors. During these trips I also met with many local and international socially oriented organizations such as multi-laterals, development banks and local foundations. As I said earlier, I spent more than ten years in Indonesia. I led a team that built what was at the time the largest retailer in Asia outside of Japan, using some of Prahalad's sales and marketing techniques for the bottom of the pyramid. This was before Prahalad wrote the seminal work on the subject. Perhaps that is why I find Prahalad's book so insightful.

Business models provide a formal process to commercialize a product in order to build a business. Therefore, this process can be applied to any commercial organization including an SEV. Inherent in the development of the business model concept is the objective that one is trying to build a large company. A large company cannot be achieved without scaling and through the scaling the SEV addresses a social problem in a significant way and perhaps on a worldwide scale.

The concept of "business model" probably originated with the case method at Harvard Business School. Business model thinking became popular with business schools, venture capital firms and startup executives in 2010 with the release of Alexander Osterwalder's *Business Model Generation: A Handbook for Visionaries, Game Changers, and Challengers.* The same year I published my first book, *Billion Dollar Company: An entrepreneur's guide to business models for high growth companies*, which presented my thinking on business models. Osterwalder and my thinking on business model overlap in several areas and in certain areas we diverge. The terminology used below to describe the parts of a business model is a combination of both sets of terms. (Note: Boston Consulting Group also has their definition of business model and Bill Aulet, the Director of the entrepreneurship center at MIT, has a new book, *Disciplined Entrepreneurship: 24 Steps to a Successful Startup*, which could be viewed as another excellent contribution to business model thinking.)

Business models provide one way to address the issue of scaling. While business models have many components, the discussion here is restricted to only those components that require special attention in scaling an SEV. The components selected in part reflect the adverse conditions in much of the third world and the lack of resources available in the local marketplaces. The business model components are:

- Partners
- Customer segments
- Sales strategy
- Distribution
- Pricing
- Value proposition
- Capital
- Human resources
- Competition

Partners

Partners take many forms in a business model, including suppliers, distributors and resource providers. Here, however, I am using the term to refer to joint venture partners, perhaps not necessarily in the legal sense but more in a "cooperative" sense of shared objectives. These local partners help to execute the solution to the social problem, may or may not provide capital, and may or may not receive compensation for their services and support.

Local partners for an SEV are essential because of the scale of the worldwide problems being tackled and in order to more effectively leverage capital. Partners also provide in depth local knowledge and a network of local contacts, both of which tend to reduce mistakes and thereby conserve capital. Teach for All's worldwide network of local private sector companies is a good example. Teach for All "seeks to address educational need...through future leaders".

While the problems are worldwide, I believe that partners should be selected by country with a very suspect eye toward regional partners. If the regional partner fails to perform, the strategy has a multi-country shortcoming. Also, in my experience there are very few partners except for the multi-laterals that are effective _and_ take a regional approach to issues. However, even the multi-laterals tend to approach issues on a single country basis in all likelihood to reduce complexity by dealing with each government individually.

The potential local partners for an SEV include the following types of organizations:

1. Government
   National governments are attractive partners because they have funding for social issues, have ministries responsible for

the issue and social issues are good politics in most countries (even those with centrally controlled governments). The drawbacks to national governments are that they are huge, slow moving bureaucracies. Also, ministries and presidents do not always agree on priorities and corruption is frequently an issue because of the large amounts of money involved. To avoid such issues, one alternative is a stand-alone government agency devoted to the social problem but not part of any ministry. Project Ceibal in Uruguay, which manages the highly acclaimed 1:1 learning project using OLPC laptops, is an excellent example of an independent agency. Such an agency approach to social issues is rare in my experience.

An alternative to the federal government in large countries (e.g. Mexico, Brazil, etc.) is to work with state or municipal governments. My experience is that this level of government is more responsive than the federal government to the social problems of the populous and better able to manage the smaller projects their responsibility covers. However, this strategy only works if the local government has responsibility for the social issue and funding that is independent of the federal government to solve the problem. To illustrate this point, in Mexico the national government has responsibility for primary schools and the state governments have responsibility for secondary schools. To do a project in primary schools typically involves the national government in Mexico.

Based on my experience, in large countries one is better off avoiding federal governments for social projects. In smaller countries, or in countries with centrally controlled governments, there may be no choice other than the federal government with which to partner.

2. Local foundations

   Local non-profits exist in most countries and can be excellent partners because of their in depth local knowledge of the social issue and their vast networks within the government and private sector. The one drawback of many local foundations is that they have limited discretionary funds to put into new projects. One way around this problem is to create a new local foundation that raises funds solely to do the project of the SEV. This approach worked well for OLPC in several countries.

3. Private sector companies

   Traditionally, many SEVs and non-profits tend to avoid partnering with private sector companies. However, if you need a showcase project to demonstrate the effectiveness of your solution to a social problem, private companies can be attractive partners because they have budget for social projects (and an increasing sense of social responsibility). An attractive feature of multi-nationals as a local partner is that a good project in one country can be adopted by a subsidiary of a multi-national in another country. For example, P&G tends to theme its social responsibility activities on a continent wide basis, with education the social issue in Latin America. Also, the private sector is sometimes willing to match funding with the government for social projects. It is much easier to get government funding if a private sector company underwrites fifty percent of the cost.

4. Universities

   Universities are overlooked as potential partners. They frequently have interested experts on local social issues and are looking for ways to provide their students hands on experience and higher quality community service. Funding may be an issue, but if one brings the funding for the project, local universities should be considered as partners. (Did I mention I teach at three universities.)

5. Faith-based Organizations

   Around the world most religious organizations devote considerable time, energy and capital to working on social issues. In some countries a religious organization may operate multiple orphanages, schools and feeding programs. Also, certain faiths have a "sympathetic" funding source, such as the Islamic Development Bank. Religious communities also have vast local networks. The challenge with religious partners is that they have their own priorities and strategies, which may not match your objectives.

6. Multi-laterals

   Equal in popularity with national governments as a partner for social projects are the multi-laterals—the UN, World Bank, etc. While all of these organizations have world headquarters, I recommend approaching them locally in order to determine their priorities in the particular country. The multi-laterals have vast experience in managing social projects, but in my experience their expertise is narrow and limited to certain social issues depending on the multi-lateral. For example, Inter-American Development Bank has extensive experience with education projects, but the World Bank and the Asian Development Bank have built up more expertise on developing capital markets.

An important consideration in partnering with multi-laterals is that they almost always require formal evaluations of their projects. I have seen the UNDP do its own evaluation, but typically the SEV is expected to define and pay the cost of an evaluation. One is advised to have thought out a complete approach to evaluation before getting deeply involved with a multi-lateral.

Dealing with partners is a time consuming task. In her book "Expanding the Pie" Susan Rae Ross states that research on cross-sector collaboration shows that it requires forty percent more time. With the additional time comes additional expense. Except for an SEV partnering with a local for-profit company or perhaps a non-profit foundation, the SEV will be in the cross-sector environment partnering with governments, faith-based organizations and universities and should expect the slower timeline Ross predicts.

Customer Segments

A customer segment is the particular group of target customers for which the product/solution solves a problem and fills a need. For example, the Dropbox customer segment might be "connected consumers who need backup and synchronization across multiple computing devices".

Typically the three possible customer segments for an SEV are:

1. Government
2. End user (individuals)
3. Collective groups such as unions, cooperatives, etc.

The tendency for social organizations is to choose a segment based on the size of the respective financial resources, with government (coffers) as the default choice. However, as Prahalad makes clear, customizing a product and its pricing to match the individuals at the bottom of the pyramid brings together both capitalism and a solution to a social problem for the purchaser. A local for-profit partner combined with the end users (individuals) as the customer segment can be a viable strategy.

Collective groups, such as unions and cooperatives, are another alternative for customer segment. They have financial resources and typically devote effort to improving the well being of their members and their families. Unions may see a social project as a way to provide more sophisticated training and development for their members. Cooperatives organized around a particular agricultural commodity also commonly have social programs. Frequently these social programs target the children of agricultural workers because their father or mother's traditional jobs may intentionally be phased out and the children need to be prepared for an alternative future. While it is doubtful that a collective group would provide national coverage for a social project, in certain countries significant penetration can be achieved which may attract other parties interested in additional market segments. Micro-finance organizations may be another form of collective to consider. The individual borrowers purchase the product from an SEV and then turnaround and sell it to the end user individual copying the Living Goods model mentioned earlier.

Sales Strategy

To quote many, "the world is a big place". There are approximately 180 developing countries of which sixty are the least developed. In considering a sales strategy to permit an SEV to scale, the first issue is to forsake the notion of addressing the entire world market simultaneously. It is more effective to begin by targeting a single region, which may be a continent such as South America or a portion of a continent such as sub-Saharan Africa. In such cases, there tends to be a high degree of social and cultural homogeneity in the targeted customer segment. These characteristics facilitate product-market fit and sales traction. A regional focus also capitalizes on the natural competition between countries, both at the government and private sector levels. Even for social projects, countries face competitive pressure to match their neighbors in terms of social services. This competitive pressure helps to accelerate the SEV's commercial and social objectives. For example, Uruguay's success with Project Ceibal prompted its larger neighbors Brazil and Argentina to start 1:1 educational computing projects.

Having selected a target region to begin, the next decision is whether to position sales people in the region or use a centralized headquarters' sales staff. I have found that locally situated sales people can be more effective, particularly when they work for independent local firms in an industry "related" to the social problem. A local sales force gives the SEV 24/7 coverage of the customer and a local partner selling gives the SEV instant market knowledge and "business" relationships.

 A good example of the value of a network of local selling partners comes from Intel. The Intel Classmate was sold by local computer manufacturers to governments for 1:1

projects in primary schools. OLPC generally used a centralized selling staff based at headquarters locations. The Classmate outsold the OLPC laptop approximately 5:1 through 2012 despite a higher price of $40-100 per laptop for arguably comparable products. I attribute the success of the Classmate in part to the local selling partners of Intel. Others might cite additional factors to explain the success of the Classmate. Of course, I do not mean to criticize OLPC in any way. They established the worldwide market for educational computers and 3.0 million children and their families directly benefited from this effort. I merely make the comparison to illustrate the point.

Distribution

Distribution is the delivery of a product from the producer to the end user. In certain industries and projects some might call this logistics. Many SEVs involved in hunger, education, healthcare, shelter and the environment face the problem of distribution in the developing world. In my experience solving the distribution problem is one of the biggest challenges for an SEV. For example, developing country governments outside their military rarely have any resources and infrastructure for distribution. Frequently a government has to rely on private sector companies for distribution, but such general distribution services are not so common in Africa and parts of Asia and add to the cost of the solution.

One innovative solution for distribution comes from Africa. In Zambia ColaLife, an unaffiliated UK non-profit, is using the local Coca Cola bottler to distribute medicine to Coca Cola's most remote retailers and then ColaLife uses paid local bicycle riders to carry medicine to nearby clinics and hospitals. Another example comes from my time in Indonesia. When Asian currencies significantly devalued in 1997, many people were no longer able to afford food and began eating tree leaves. The Australian government realized the problem and offered food relief to the Indonesian government. Concerned by issues over the security of the food, the Australian government turned to our publicly traded retail company to distribute the food. I have also found local World Food Program branches to be a willing no cost distributor for food and non-food products that can be effectively distributed through local schools.

There are solutions to the distribution problem in the developing world, but the solutions frequently involve new and novel approaches. Local private companies with social responsibility programs can frequently be attractive distribution partners. One industry group on a worldwide basis that can help with distribution is the cellular carriers, who typically serve even the poorest people in developing countries and have secure, nationwide distribution networks.

Value Proposition

A value proposition is the unique [competitive] set of economic and emotional benefits of a product or service such that a target customer enters into an economic exchange. A value proposition is a fundamental concept in all forms of entrepreneurship including social entrepreneurship and the foundation for achieving scale. In the developing world correctly identifying the needs of the people, which leads to formulating the emotional and economic benefits, can be particularly challenging. Three examples illustrate the point.

1. In India an SEV built modern medical diagnostic facilities to serve large, poor communities at an affordable price. Sales were below budget until the company realized that "witch doctors"[16] were successfully competing for diagnostic services. This SEV was owned and operated by local Indians and still missed the emotional relationship, the trust, between the sick and the witch doctors.

2. In Africa farmers were offered free seeds that would significantly increase crop yield and family cash flow. Few farmers were willing to use the new seeds because if the

seeds did not perform as promised the farmers' families might starve to death. Turned out only farmers with a fourth grade education or better could properly assess the risk-return benefits of the new seeds.

3. OLPC promoted itself worldwide as a learning or education project. Government sponsors who did the three largest OLPC projects cited social inclusion rather than improving education as the motivating factor.

I think the biggest risk to successfully defining a value proposition is the untested assumption or more precisely what we in the developed world take for granted. For example, without electricity one assumes that a manually rechargeable battery is an attractive feature. Problem solvers living at the BOP have many other alternative ways to re-charge batteries. The assumption to include a rechargeable battery may result in increased product cost with no appreciable benefit to the end user and render the product un-saleable.

Frog Design, one of the leading design firms in the world, offers their services to social projects around the world. Frog has developed a step-by-step process that they use in the developing world to properly identify customer need. This process is explained in detail at http://www.frogdesign.com/collective-action-toolkit. A variation on the Frog approach that I also like is design thinking as taught at the Stanford Design School and popularized by IDEO.

In addition to the additional complexity in properly identifying the customer need, social projects including SEVs need to recognize that they have a greater requirement to educate their customers. Needs and benefits have to be explained in terms that the local people can appreciate. Frequently education is required before the target user can appreciate a need and a solution. For example, it is difficult to understand why you should take medicine if you have never been exposed to the concept of curing or preventing a disease.

Competition

Social projects, particularly SEVs, have competition not only for end users but also for partners and distributors. Ivan Krstic, TR35 Laureate and former OLPC employee, states the problem well, "altruism has a credibility problem in an industry that thrives on intense commercial competition". For example, there are multiple providers of children's laptops, solar rechargers and water purification equipment. As the SEV starts to achieve scale, traditional for-profit companies are attracted to the market. The competitors can bring world-class sales and marketing teams, significant corporate social responsibility funds and budgets for travel to international conferences to influence government officials. They also have well developed logistics systems to support local manufacturing, which is attractive to government's concerned about job creation. For example, Microsoft and Intel both competed with OLPC in educational computing. The annual marketing funds expended by the two multi-nationals for educational computing is estimated to be $400 million per year, several multiples of OLPC's annual revenue.

The question is how to respond to the inevitable competition. One approach is to embrace the competitors because they are also providing a solution to the social problem, which is presumably the key objective of the SEV. The other alternative is to see them as a threat to the sustainability of the SEV, as every sale they make deprives the SEV of a sale and the related cash flow. I believe there are many benefits to embracing the competition, but such an approach should be part of the initial thinking about the SEV rather than a later stage decision. If the SEV can use an existing commercial product or a product modified to lower the cost, then the SEV saves product development cost and can piggy-back on the sales, marketing and distribution resources of, for example, a large multi-national. The challenges in such an approach are two-fold:

1. The multi-national needs to be convinced that there is a market for the new, cheaper product variation which can be very challenging given that the market may not yet be documented (Christensen has written extensively on this challenge.) This lack of documentation for a market is the reason OLPC could not find an established computer manufacturer and ended up manufacturing themselves through Quanta Computers in Taiwan.

2. The multi-national product may not be a "perfect" solution to the social issue, which forces the SEV to make hard decisions between access to greater resources from the multi-national partner or preserving the SEV's ideological beliefs.
Having witnessed the effects of world-class competitors on the results of a comparatively successful SEV, I would recommend that an SEV be willing to modify its expectations for the scope of social benefits (ideology) in order to achieve a partnership with a likely future multi-national competitor.

Capital

I have spent much of my career involved in finance, as a banker with Chase Manhattan Bank in Latin America, raising $600 million dollars to support the growth of the retail company in Indonesia and later raising money for companies in the Caribbean and Central America. My experience, and many discussions with entrepreneurs in developing countries, suggests that the single biggest problem in developing countries is access to capital through loans and equity investment. An SEV looking to address a worldwide problem should plan to use its own financial resources because capital is a significant constraint for partners in the developing world.

Another factor that strains capital resources for the SEV is working capital requirements, particularly for an SEV with a product as opposed to one delivering services. Manufacturing lead times, trans-Pacific shipping and the time to receive customer payment can result in an SEV having to finance inventory for 8-10 months before receiving payment.

Another capital requirement related to product is the cost of new product development. A for-profit competitor to the SEV is quick to introduce new products, quicker to say the SEV product is out of date and may be fond of telling the prospective buyers that the poor little SEV lacks the capital to provide post-sale product support. Particularly in an intensely competitive, innovative market segment such as personal computing, the SEV needs to plan for ongoing capital requirements to fund new product development.

Another challenge in managing an SEV is gauging the value capture in the pricing to achieve sustainability. Easier access to capital provides more flexibility in the event that revenues do not match forecast, cash flow breakeven is delayed for a variety of traditional reasons or the costs for market entry are underestimated.

The simple solution to the capital problem is to organize the SEV as a for-profit company as opposed to a non-profit foundation. Non-profits without a large, recurring base of donors, in my experience, have little chance to secure significant working capital finance from commercial banks. A for-profit SEV has access to commercial banks, equity investors and even an IPO. Access to capital is the most critical challenge to scaling in my experience. For-profit status permits access to capital markets and generally far out ways the benefits of non-profit status for an organization tackling a worldwide social problem.

William Duggan[17] also provides a useful insight that again argues for an SEV to be a for-profit. Every organization needs to adjust their strategy for the realities of their environment, whether it is economic, competitive or technological considerations. Donative non-profits typically raise their monies based on a mission statement. If the mission statement needs to change due to "market" feedback, the original donors may no longer be willing to fund the change in strategy because of their interest in a particular mission. For example, a non-profit that develops software for a particular medical diagnosis using a cell phone might not be able to raise donations to develop their own diagnostic device if competitive conditions suggested such a change in strategy. In addition to limited availability of funding through commercial markets, non-profits may be constrained in their access to capital by their original mission statement.

Human Resources

The people and the culture of many social projects are different from for-profit companies. Rarely, in my experience, are socially motivated people interested in only one social issue and frequently are concerned about a wide variety of social issues. Case in point, I know of a social venture to build wind turbines for electricity in Africa that was criticized by its internal staff because the wind turbines killed birds. I am quite confident in saying that General Motors' staff has never had a discussion about the number of birds killed each year by Chevrolets.

Social projects have a tendency to expand their mission to a wider set of social issues, which can confuse focus, slow implementation and lead to more costly operations. I believe that a social project such as an SEV is better served to focus on a single issue unless there is no marginal cost to expand the scope of the social issues.

Another common practice is for social projects to pay staff below market salaries and benefits because the project is "doing good". My experience, and I acknowledge exceptions, is that people who work for below market compensation tend to be below market performers. I recommend that a social project hire the best people available at market rates. They are equally motivated to achieve the mission because they are professionals, typically more experienced and efficient and require less management oversight. In the long run better staff is less costly than lesser staff. Performance-based incentives can be used to offer employees an upside.

Another framework to understand the challenges of scaling an SEV is presented in "Identifying the Drivers of Social Entrepreneurial Impact" by Paul Bloom and Brett Smith[18]. The article identifies seven capabilities an organization needs to achieve scale on social ventures:

1. Staffing--"the effectiveness of the organization at filling its labor needs, including its managerial posts, with people who have the requisite skills for the needed positions, whether they be paid staff or volunteers"

2. Communicating--"the effectiveness with which the organization is able to persuade key stakeholders that its change strategy is worth adopting and/or supporting"

3. Alliance building--" the effectiveness with which the organization has forged partnerships, coalitions, joint ventures, and other linkages to bring about desired social changes"

4. Lobbying--"the effectiveness with which the organization is able to advocate for government actions that may work in its favor"

5. Earnings generation--"the effectiveness with which the organization generates a stream of revenue that exceeds its expenses"

6. Replicating--"the effectiveness with which the organization can reproduce the programs and initiatives that it has originated"

7. Stimulating market force--"the effectiveness with which the organization can create incentives that encourage people or institutions to pursue private interests while also serving the public good"

While I think that this framework under estimates the importance of access to capital for scaling by its implied self-reliance on internally generated cash flow [5], the framework makes two closely related points that I have not explicitly discussed:

- Persuading key stakeholders that its strategy is worth adopting
- Replicating programs and initiatives

With the increased awareness of social issues, the increased funding for corporate social responsibility, and the focus on social entrepreneurship by universities around the world, the competition for stakeholders and financial sponsors has gotten much more intense. Many such supporters have become more sophisticated in how they choose their social projects and have adopted formal programs to evaluate new and existing projects. With these formal processes comes a requirement for new projects to demonstrate positive outcomes from previous projects. This focus on previous evaluations is an explicit concern not only with outcomes but also with the question of whether results can be replicated in new communities. In my experience, previous evaluations are increasingly becoming the key factor in persuading a stakeholder to adopt a social program [2].

In order to successfully achieve a replicable business model for an SEV requires focus on three key elements:

1. Partner selection
2. Distribution
3. Access to capital

The successful SEV should be looking for a type of partner and method of distribution that is widely available around the world, where the self-interest of such partner(s) is served by participating in the social project. Different types of partners and distributors in each new community or country force the SEV to incur the costly expense of a new learning curve for each project. While the tendency may be to conclude that there is no partner available or a sufficiently skilled organization to partner with in multiple countries, it is much more capital efficient to keep analyzing the types of partners available until you find an attractive type, rather than to keep doing one off business models. Of course, my approach would be to look for private sector partners and distributors who are generally available in every country or can be trained sufficiently well at a comparatively low cost.

While these partners may provide a higher cost solution given their profit motive, they most likely would not engage in the project if they thought they were priced out of the market and could not achieve meaningful scale. These local partners are better able to judge the cost that the local market will bear for a solution. The wide spread availability of the solution to the social problem is more important than the end user cost of the solution. It is not the purpose of the SEV or any other social organization to dictate how a poor family spends their money but rather to offer solutions where the family sees it in their self-interest to make a purchase. This is the basic economic tenet of a self-interested exchange, provided the economic returns to the provider are not in excess of standard commercial norms.

Before the reader takes issue with this line of reasoning, I would like to point out that Unus' micro-finance project charged its borrowers 40 percent interest, well in excess of local bank loan rates in Bangladesh. Rather than being concerned with what some might consider "usurious" interest rates, Unus let the prospective borrowers decide whether the rate was appropriate and the success of that decision is well documented by the many, many successful micro-finance projects around the world.

Chapter VIII- Conclusions

Much of the world already has access to food, water, healthcare and shelter. These social benefits were to a large degree provided by for-profit companies. *The Economist* estimates that approximately one billion people escaped poverty in the twenty-year period ending in 2010 through the benefits of capitalism.[19] This level of impact in poverty eradication supports both the notion that for-profit activities address social problems and that such approaches scale. The only difference between an SEV and a for-profit is in the expectations for how value is shared between the end users and the shareholders. (Such decisions may or may not affect the pace of change or the rate of scaling.) The sharing of value is effectively a decision on how the value proposition is defined with no need for normative judgments. The target market, explicit in every value proposition, provides the flexibility to select the poor, the indigenous or the disadvantaged--again with no need for a normative judgment. However, in picking such large markets to address, the critical resource becomes capital. Capital markets are best accessed by electing for-profit status and avoiding the restrictions today of non-profit status.

Some of my students think that I do not like social entrepreneurship. This conclusion is to misunderstand me. I believe that social entrepreneurship is a viable alternative required to help address the large social problems. I just believe that social entrepreneurship does not require normative judgments. A group of people that are poor or indigenous is served just as well, whether we think of them as "deserving" or simply as a market. If traditional capitalists and entrepreneurs were perhaps more enlightened, we would have less debate about the morality of capitalism, much quicker solutions to worldwide social problems and perhaps even no need for the distinction of "social" entrepreneurship.

Looking ahead I see two important results from social entrepreneurship beyond the improved social outcomes:

1. The increased use of social entrepreneurship and its success will make more people, and even government officials, realize that government is not the default solution provider for social problems. The private sector can expand its role in solving social problems.
2. For the private sector to expand its role in addressing social problems business schools and related institutions must realize and teach business in such a way that social considerations are part of initial corporate planning and not

just a public relations strategy. The increased use of the social entrepreneurship business model will demonstrate this type of thinking and encourage educational institutions to make the necessary changes in curriculum and thinking. Early research from institutions such as Harvard Business School is showing that more socially aware companies provide better shareholder returns. Now if Toms Shoes would just do an IPO for its new private equity investors, the full range of economic and social benefits from social entrepreneurship would be demonstrated. This event might demonstrate a new way for people to think about entrepreneurship and capitalism and accelerate the change in the way business is taught. In the end to demonstrate the morality of capitalism we must teach the students a better model and social entrepreneurship offers many of those lessons.

Robert Hacker

Miami, FL

December 2014

Rhhfla@gmail,com

Footnotes

[1] Porter, Michael E. and Kramer, Mark R.(October 2011), Creating Social Value, Harvard Business Review
[2] Macomber, John D., (Summer 2011), The Role of Finance and Private Investment in Developing Sustainable Cities, Journal of Applied Corporate Finance 23, no. 3
[3] Concurring Opinions (2012), http://www.concurringopinions.com/
[4] Caldwell, Bruce, 2004, Hayek's Challenge: An Intellectual Biography of F.A. Hayek, The University of Chicago Press
[5] Wikipedia
[6] Hansmann, Henry, (1987), Economic Theories of Non-profit Organizations, The Nonprofit Sector A Research Handbook Volume: 1,Yale University Press
[7] National Center for Charitable Statistics http://nccsdataweb.urban.org/NCCS/V1Pub/index.php
[8] Brigitte Hoogendoorn (2011) A Conceptual Overview of What We Know About Social Entrepreneurship, EIM Research Reports
[9] J. Gregory Dees, The Meaning of "Social Entrepreneurship", 1998
[10] Santos, Filipe M. (2009), A Positive Theory of Social Entrepreneurship, INSEAD Working Paper
[11] This view of society is derived from the writings of F.A. Hayek, who may have derived it from the works of earlier economists or philosophers.
[12] In certain circumstances value creation may include value created for partners and suppliers. Basically, any marginal utility created increases value created.
[13] Santos, Filipe M. (2009), A Positive Theory of Social Entrepreneurship. INSEAD Working Paper
[14] If an SEV such as TOMS Shoes were to do an IPO, it may turn out that an SEV can achieve market rates of return for investors, but I know of no publicly available information to document investor returns in SEVs. Anecdotal information

suggests current returns are at below market rates.

[15] http://www.nextbillion.net/blogpost.aspx?blogid=3409

[16] I mean no offense to local, indigenous medical advisors with no modern, formal training in medicine by referring to them as witch doctors. Maybe I just watched too many Tarzan movies as a child.

[17] Duggan, William (2007), Strategic Intuition, Columbia Business School Publishing

[18] Paul Bloom and Brett Smith (March 2010), Identifying the Drivers of Social Entrepreneurial Impact, Journal of Social Entrepreneurship Vol. 1, No. 1, 126–145

[19] http://www.economist.com/news/leaders/21578665-nearly-1-billion-people-have-been-taken-out-extreme-poverty-20-years-world-should-aim